God Made Me Special, Just Like You!

By Nicki Olin

Halo
Publishing International

ISBN 13: 978-1-61244-061-3
Library of Congress Control Number: 2012902566

Printed in the United States of America

Halo ● ● ● ●
Publishing International
www.halopublishing.com

Published by Halo Publishing International
AP·726
P.O. Box 60326
Houston, Texas 77205
Toll Free 1-877-705-9647
www.halopublishing.com
www.holapublishing.com
e-mail: contact@halopublishing.com

This book is for my amazing daughter Brooklyn, I hope you always know how beautiful you are! I love you so much!

- Mommy

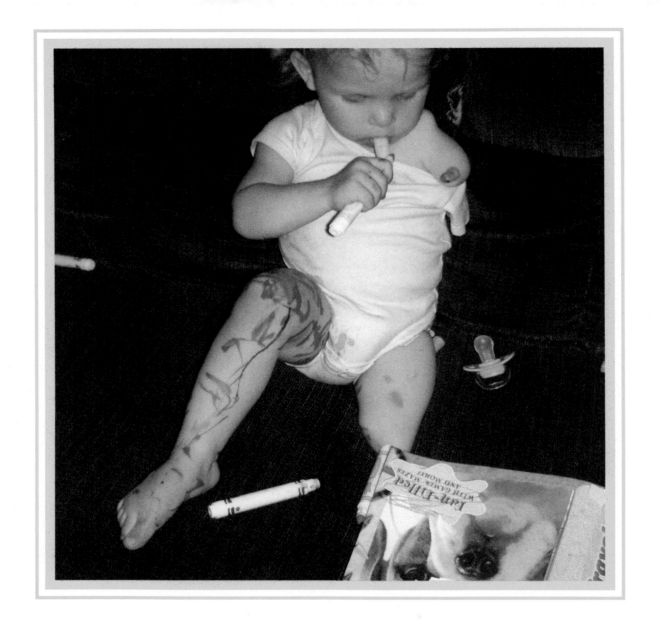

I may look different as you can clearly see,

God made some parts unique on me!

I have a little left arm and a little left leg,

 B ut I do not walk on just a wood peg.

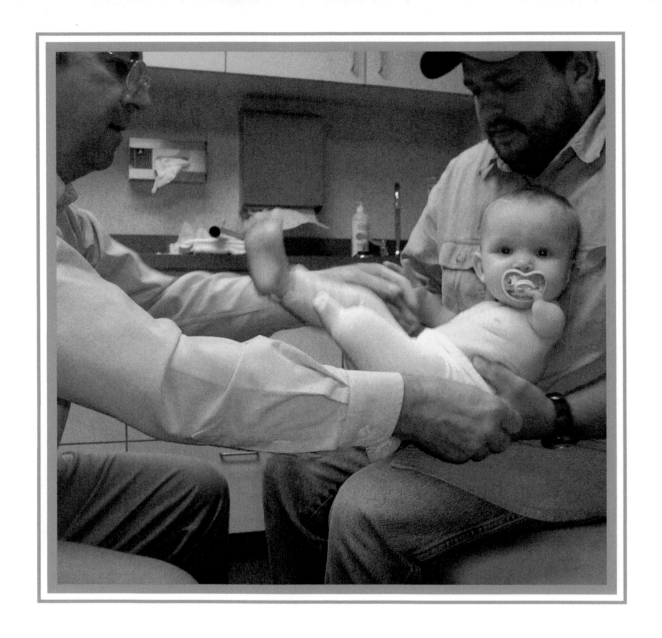

I have these friends named Patrick and Dave,
they always greet me with a smile and a wave.

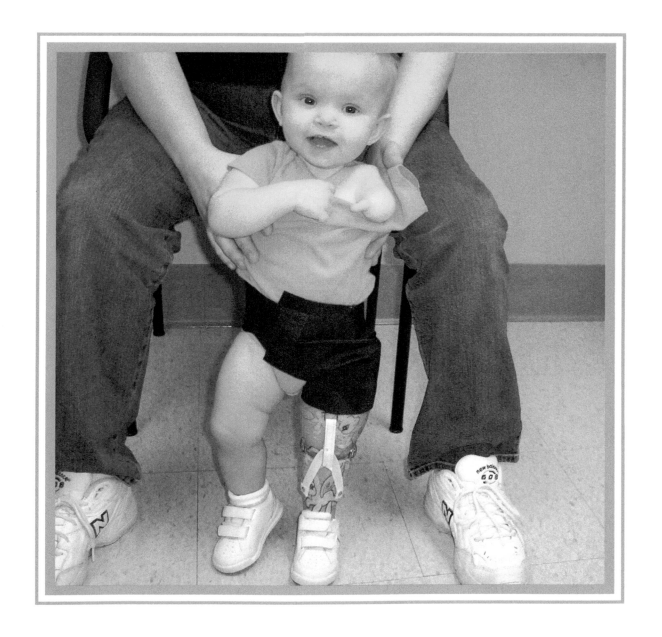

They make me my special and beautiful leg,
I get a toy when I see them, I don't even beg!

If my leg is too short, they make it tall.
They tell me be careful, but I run and don't fall!

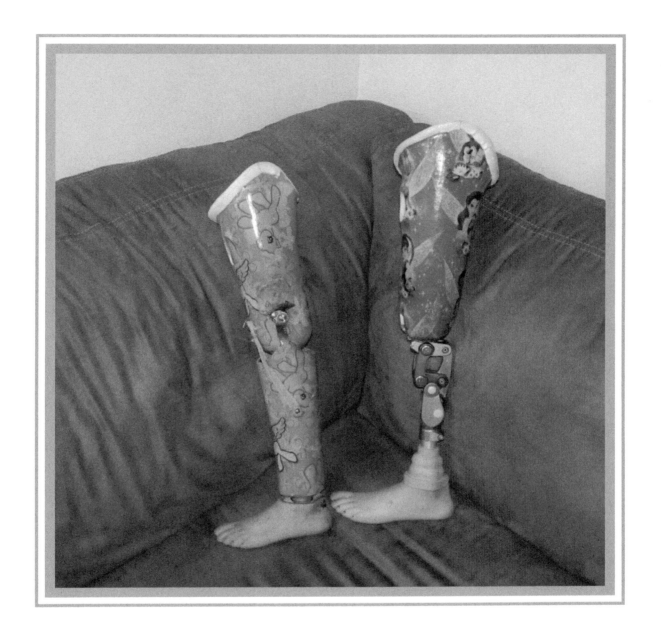

If I grow too much they have to make me a new one.
But I think that is a whole lot of fun!

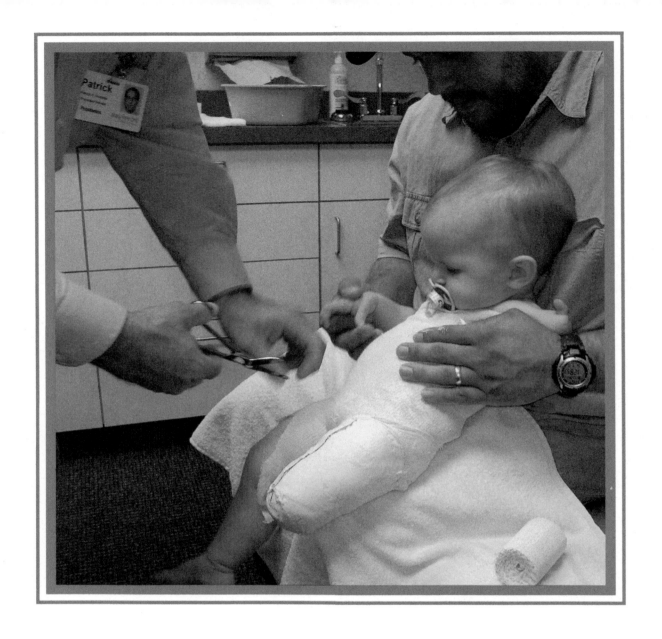

They have to measure and cast.
It all goes pretty fast.

I can choose whatever design that I like,
I can even get something that matches my bike!

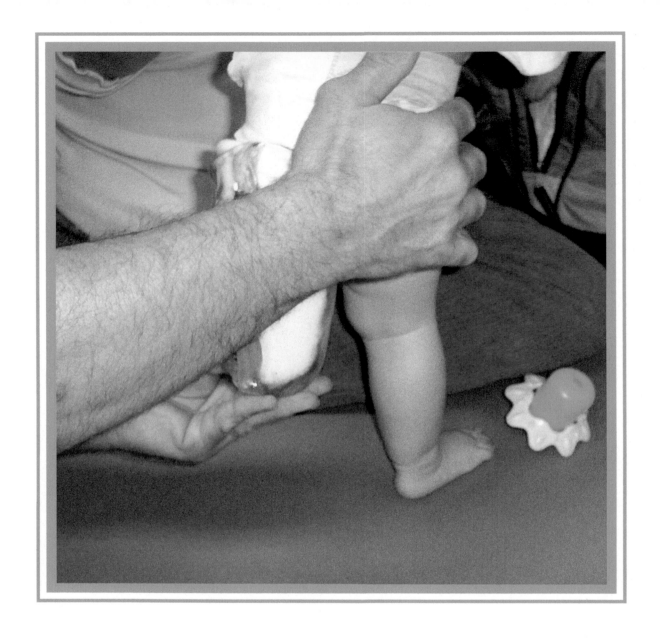

It takes them a few weeks to put it all together.
It's not really that long but it seems like forever!

I get my new leg and it feels so great!
It fits me just perfect, there is no debate.

My prosthetic leg helps me run, jump and play.

I usually take it off at the end of the day.

I have one little finger on my tiny left arm,
some people look with surprise and alarm.

Some kids ask about it and some like to feel.
My baby sister seems to think it's a meal!

My little finger is awesome, I use it so much!
I use it to feel and to hold and to touch!

My body may look different to you,
but there is still a lot that I CAN do!

I can zip my own coat with one hand by myself.

I can carry a whole stack of books to the shelf.

I can do all the things that my friends like to do.
Come on, let's go! I will play with you too!

Thank you God for making me perfect as can be.
I have great friends and family and they all love me!

God made all of us special in one way or another. We want to know what makes you special. With help from your parents, go to God Made Me Special, Just Like You on facebook and tell us your story.

God Made Me Special, Just Like You!
By Nicki Olin

Book Order Form

E-mail Orders:
timnickikids@aol.com
Website Orders:
www.halopublishing.com

Mail To:
Nicki Olin, author
4386 E. 104th Street
Grant, MI 49327

Shipping:
U.S. $3.50 first book
$2.00 for each additonial

God Made Me Special, Just Like You!
By Nicki Olin

Name:_____

Address:_____

City:_____ State:_____ Zip Code:_____

Telephone:_____Personalized to:_____

Qty. ____ *God Made Me Special, Just Like You!* $12.95 Total $_____

Shipping and Handling $_____

Your City Tax $_____

Total Amount Enclosed $_____

CPSIA information can be obtained
at www.ICGtesting.com
Printed in the USA
BVOW10s0921281216

472038BV00016B/278/P